Molly Bannaky

For my husband, Marion McGill,
and my daughters, Gwendolyn and Paulette
—A. M.

I dedicate this book to all the teachers in the world
for their tireless and compassionate efforts to educate our future.
Thank you.
—C. K. S.

Text copyright © 1999 by Alice McGill
Illustrations copyright © 1999 by Chris Soentpiet

The text of this book is set in 14-point Minion Semibold.
The illustrations are watercolor on illustration board.

Library of Congress Cataloging-in-Publication Data

McGill, Alice.
Molly Bannaky / by Alice McGill; illustrated by Chris Soentpiet.
p. cm.
Summary: Relates how Benjamin Banneker's grandmother journeyed from England to Maryland in the late
seventeenth century, worked as an indentured servant, began a farm of her own, and married a freed slave.
ISBN 0-395-72287-X
1. Banneker, Benjamin, 1731–1806—Family—Juvenile fiction.
[1. Banneker, Benjamin, 1731–1806—Family—Fiction. 2. Farm life—Fiction.] I. Soentpiet, Chris, ill. II. Title.
PZ7.M478468Ban 1999
[E]—dc20 96-3000 CIP AC

Manufactured in the United States of America
WOZ 10 9 8 7 6 5

Molly Bannaky

written by **Alice McGill**   *pictures by* **Chris K. Soentpiet**

HOUGHTON MIFFLIN COMPANY

BOSTON

On a cold, gray morning in 1685, Molly Walsh sat on a stool, tugging at the udder of an obstinate cow. She was a dairymaid, and it was her duty to get up every morning around five o'clock and go to that same shed and milk that same cow. The man who owned the cow owned the cottage where she lived, the manor house, and all the land around. He was lord.

Molly kept tugging. The milk squirted into the pail. When the pail was full, it was her duty to take it up the hill to the manor house and hand it to the scullery maid, who handed it to the kitchen maid, who handed it to the cook. The jittery cow kept hooking its head. The week before, the cow had kicked over her pail of milk. The cook had warned Molly that she would be brought before the court if ever again she stole his lordship's milk. That was the law.

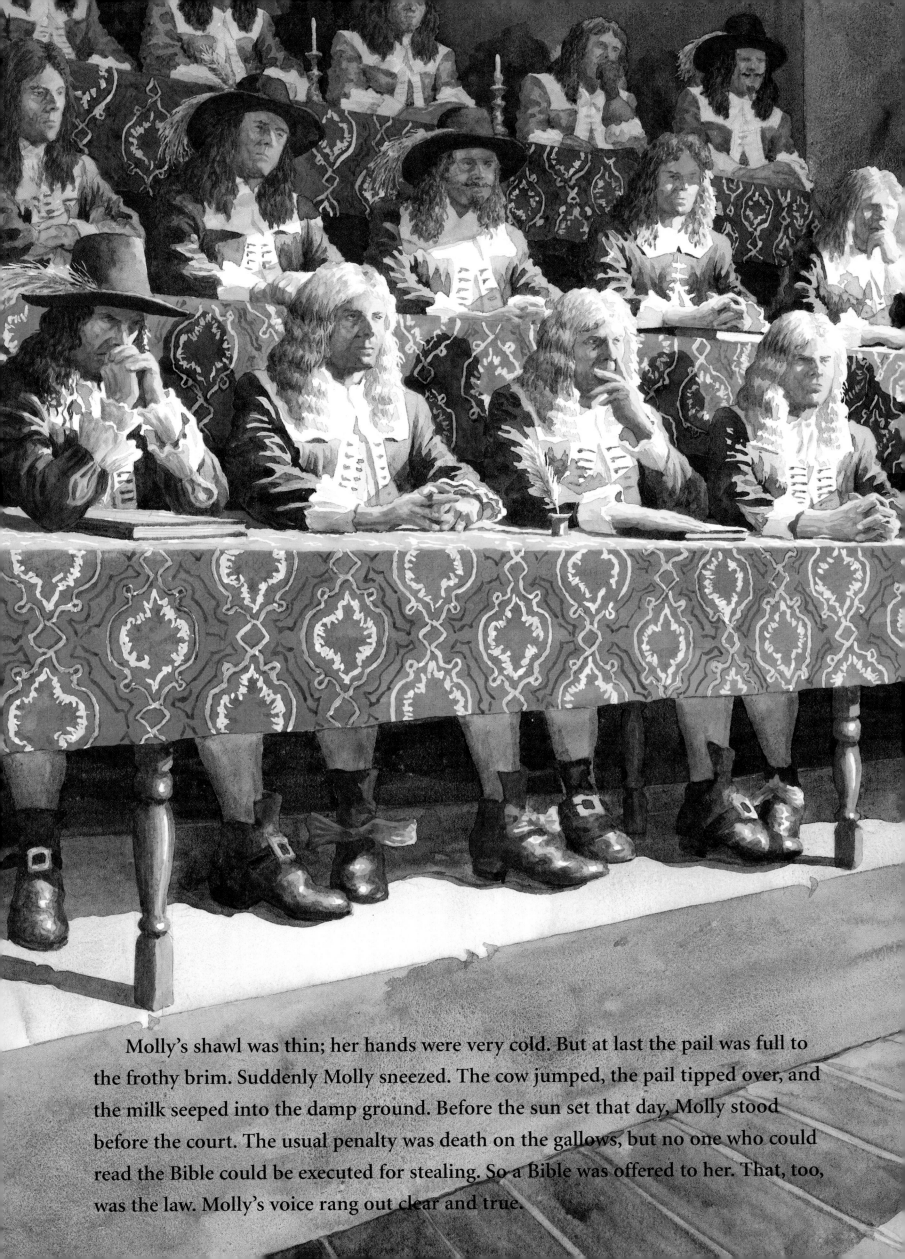

Molly's shawl was thin; her hands were very cold. But at last the pail was full to the frothy brim. Suddenly Molly sneezed. The cow jumped, the pail tipped over, and the milk seeped into the damp ground. Before the sun set that day, Molly stood before the court. The usual penalty was death on the gallows, but no one who could read the Bible could be executed for stealing. So a Bible was offered to her. That, too, was the law. Molly's voice rang out clear and true.

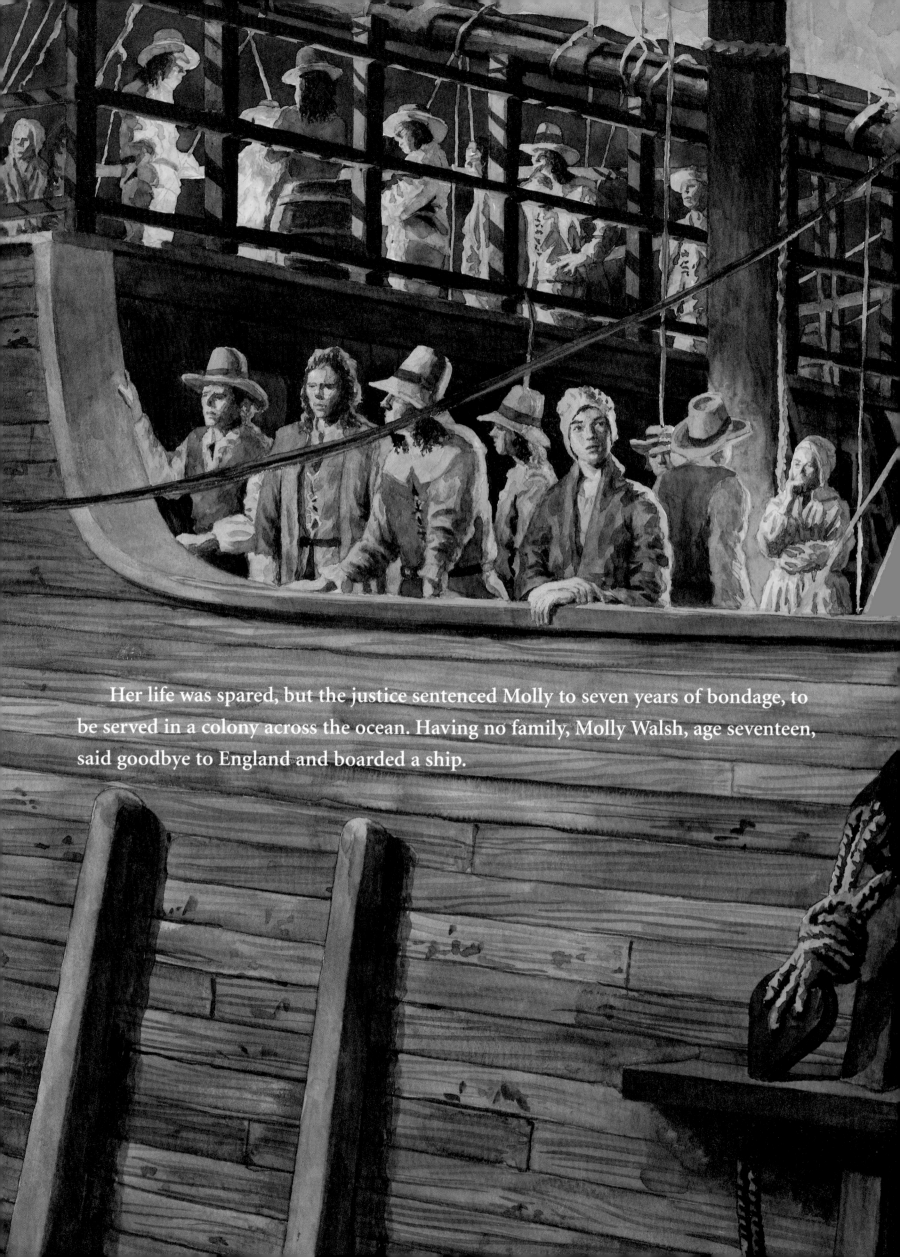

Her life was spared, but the justice sentenced Molly to seven years of bondage, to be served in a colony across the ocean. Having no family, Molly Walsh, age seventeen, said goodbye to England and boarded a ship.

After she landed in the New World, Molly worked for a planter on the eastern
shore of Maryland. There the cannons fired at daybreak, calling the servants to work.
Molly tended her master's tobacco crops, pressing the tiny brown seeds into the earth
and picking the worms from the flowering stalks. Her callused hands grew strong
enough to control a team of oxen and to hold the plow steady. In her spare time,
Molly sewed and nursed the sick for pay.

After working for the planter for seven years, Molly was free to go. As the law required, the farmer gave her an ox hitched to a cart, a plow, two hoes, a bag of tobacco seeds, a bag of seed corn, clothing, and a gun. Acres and acres of fertile land stretched ahead of her. Just before sunset that same day, Molly left the road and went four miles into the wilderness, where she staked her claim.

That a lone woman should stake land was unheard of, but Molly's new neighbors saw the way she jutted out her chin. They helped her build a one-room cabin. They helped her harvest and cure her first crop. They helped her cart the tobacco to the warehouse to sell. But Molly soon realized that the farm was too much for her to manage alone.

One day Molly read a posted announcement that a ship would be landing soon. Because she needed help in working her land, she decided to watch the docking of this ship—a slave ship. She watched the men of Africa file by, one after the other. She saw the misery, anger, and shame on their faces as they were forced to mount the auction block. Then Molly noticed a tall, regal man who dared to look into the eyes of every bidder. Molly bought him and vowed to treat him well and set him free just as soon as her land was cleared.

Molly talked to this man, using her hands and arms to tell him of her homeland and of her years as an indentured servant. He smiled at this strange-looking woman, with sweet-grass eyes and straw hair and skin the color of the underside of a melon. He told her his name: Bannaky.

Because he was not used to the climate, he was often sick with chills and fever. Still, Bannaky would walk up and down the rows of tobacco, stopping to turn each leaf on a stalk as if reading a printed page. He showed Molly how to dig ditches to guide streams of water down the furrows.

As the tobacco ripened in the fields, Molly and Bannaky grew to love each other. She signed his freedom papers, and a traveling minister performed their marriage rites. Though Molly had broken colonial law by marrying a black man, her neighbors came to accept this marriage and to respect Bannaky. In times of drought he shared his knowledge of irrigation and crop rotation, learned at an early age in his native country.

Years passed. Molly and Bannaky had four young daughters. A large house and many outbuildings overlooked their hundred acres of land.

Suddenly a great sadness struck the family. Bannaky died, and Molly was alone again. She drew her daughters closer to her and taught them how to work the land.

In time she had a grandson, born of her eldest daughter, Mary, and her husband, Robert. In her Bible, Molly wrote her new grandson's name: Benjamin Banneker. She taught this young boy to read and write. She told him about his grandfather, a prince who was the son of a king in Africa, and about her days as a dairymaid across the ocean in England.

HISTORICAL NOTE

IN THE LATE SEVENTEENTH CENTURY, MANY PEOPLE FROM ENGLAND CHOSE TO leave the hunger and poverty of their country. They became servants in the American colonies, where laborers were desperately needed. In exchange for sea passage, indentured servants agreed to work for seven years, after which time they were declared free. Some, such as Molly Walsh, became indentured servants when they were exiled from England by law. Molly herself escaped death on the gallows by a legal loophole—she could read the Bible, and so her life was spared. It was the responsibility of the court to supply the Bible, as many poor people did not own them. Many years later, after she became a free woman, Molly purchased a Bible from England.

After a grueling two-month voyage below the decks of a ship, where crowded and unsanitary conditions often led to disease, the "seven-year passengers" were sold to owners, who were required to provide them with food, shelter, and clothing. At the end of their term, bonded servants were given "all that was needed to start again on their own." Often they moved farther west and staked claims; settlers could pay for the land after their first crop was sold. African slaves had no such options: they were treated as property for the duration of their lives.

Under their laws, colonists could be forced into slavery for marrying a slave, though Molly Bannaky was never prosecuted for this "crime." Molly also feared retribution from disapproving neighbors. Bannaky never converted to Christianity, and as the nearest church was in Baltimore, it is thought that a traveling minister married them privately. Because Bannaky was free, their four children were born free. Their eldest daughter, Mary, also married an African slave, Robert. When Robert became a baptized Christian, the planter who owned him set him free—free to marry, free to own land, free to come and go as he pleased. Having no last name, Robert took his wife's name—Bannaky. By the time their first son was born the spelling of their name had changed to Banneker.

Taught to read from his grandmother's cherished Bible, Benjamin Banneker (1731–1806) went on to become a highly regarded scientist and mathematician. He taught himself astronomy and surveying and was appointed to the federal survey commission that planned Washington, D.C. Benjamin Banneker is best known for calculating "ephemerides," tables that use the locations of the sun, moon, and stars to measure time. From the year 1792 to 1802, he published an almanac—the first by a black man—featuring these astronomical tables, as well as scientific essays. Benjamin Banneker wanted to disprove the popular belief that blacks were inferior to whites in intelligence. In 1791, he wrote to Secretary of State Thomas Jefferson concerning the injustice of slavery, enclosing one of his almanacs. Jefferson answered, agreeing with Benjamin Banneker, and sent a copy of the almanac to the Academy of Sciences in Paris.